This book
belongs to

_____

_____

WHITE STAR PUBLISHERS

CONTENTS

THE START OF THE STORY

When Mom learned that I was on the way

....

....

....

....

What Mom said to Dad

....

....

How Dad reacted

....

....

While she was waiting for me, Mom imagined me like this

....

....

....

While he was waiting for me, Dad imagined me like this

....

....

This is what Mom and Dad called me when I was still in Mom's tummy

....

....

I was expected on this day

....

The preparations completed before I arrived

....

....

IN MOM'S BIG TUMMY

My parents heard my heartbeat for the first time

....

....

....

Mom felt me kick for the first time

....

....

....

While waiting for me, Mom always had a craving for

....

....

....

My family made important preparations before my arrival, such as

....

....

....

....

....

THE FIRST ECHOGRAPH

MOM WITH BIG TUMMY

MY FAMILY

Mom's name is ....

Her dream for me is ....

....

....

....

Dad's name is ....

His dream for me is ....

....

....

....

The other members of my family ....

....

....

....

....

....

Some information about my family

MY FAMILY TREE

BROTHERS   ME   SISTERS

COUSINS   COUSINS

AUNTS - UNCLES   DAD   MOM   AUNTS - UNCLES

GRANDFATHER   GRANDMOTHER   GRANDFATHER   GRANDMOTHER

GREAT-GRANDPARENTS   GREAT-GRANDPARENTS   GREAT-GRANDPARENTS   GREAT-GRANDPARENTS

FAMILY PHOTOS

HERE I AM!

I was born on

....

At

....

My weight

....

My height

....

I came into the world at

....

The doctor and obstetrician in attendance were

....

....

Mom and Dad describe my first day like this

....

....

....

....

MY PHOTOS

WHAT THEY SAID ABOUT ME...

Mom's first words were

....

....

....

....

Dad's first words were

....

....

....

....

The reactions of my siblings, cousins, grandparents, uncles, aunts and friends

....

....

....

I also received best wishes from

....

....

....

PRECIOUS MEMENTOS

A lock of my hair

My hospital's bracelet

MY NAME

Mom's and Dad's favorite names were

....

....

The name they decided on is

They chose this name because

....

....

....

My name means

....

....

My nickname is

They call me in this way because

....

....

....

MY IDENTIKIT

My eyes ....

My hair ....

My skin color ....

....

What I got from Mom ....

....

What I got from Dad ....

....

MY PHOTOS

AN UNFORGETTABLE DATE

This is what was happening in the world when I was born

....

....

....

The headlines on the front page of the newspaper

....

....

....

The first song on the charts was

Mom and Dad's favorite singers were

....

....

The most famous actors were

....

....

Some sports champions of the time

....

....

A quart of milk cost

A newspaper cost ....

SPACE FOR NEWSPAPER ARTICLES AND OTHER MEMENTOS

HOME AT LAST!

The date I arrived at home
....

My first address
....

....

During the trip, I
....

....

....

Waiting for me at home
....

....

....

As soon as I was inside, I
....

....

....

My bedroom is decorated like this
....

....

....

Around me were gifts from persons dear to me
....

....

....

MY PHOTOS

SWEET DREAMS!

My first night at home I slept .... hours ....

And my parents slept .... hours ....

That first night they thought ....

....

....

To fall asleep I need ....

....

....

My favorite lullaby is ....

....

....

The position I sleep in ....

....

....

I can't fall asleep if ....

....

....

MY FAVORITE LULLABYES

MY PHOTOS

WAKE UP, SLEEPYHEAD!

Am I an early riser or a sleepyhead?

....

....

....

This is how I tell everyone I'm awake

....

....

....

As soon as I open my eyes, I immediately want

....

....

....

....

IT'S TIME TO EAT!

My first solid food

....

....

....

....

Mom's recipes

....

....

....

....

My favorite dish

....

....

....

....

I really don't like

....

....

....

....

I used a spoon all by myself when I was

....

MY PHOTOS

IT'S BATH TIME

My first time in water

....

....

....

....

My reactions

....

....

....

....

....

....

In the water I enjoy

....

....

....

....

....

MY PHOTOS

MY DEVELOPMENT STAGES

	WEIGHT	HEIGHT	HEAD CIRCUMFERENCE
At birth			
One month			
Two months			
Three months			
Four months			
Five months			
Six months			
Seven months			
Eight months			
Nine months			
Ten months			
Eleven months			
Twelve months			
Two years			
Three years			

Vaccinations ....

....

....

AT THE DOCTOR/BABY TEETH

central incisor

central incisor

canine

first molar

second molar

central incisor

lateral incisor

canine

first molar

second molar

upper jaw

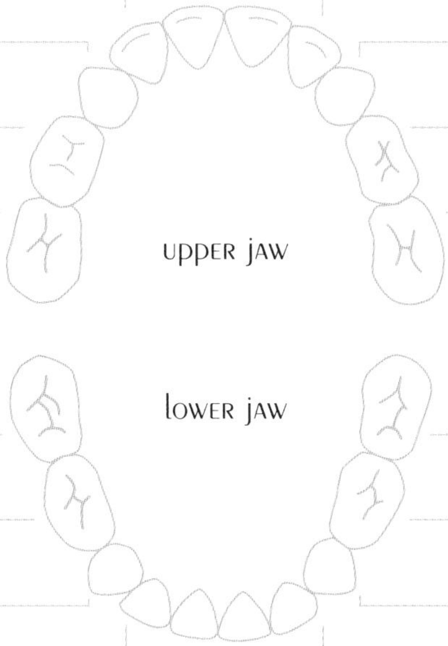

LEFT PROFILE

RIGHT PROFILE

lower jaw

second molar

first molar

canine

lateral incisor

central incisor

second molar

first molar

canine

lateral incisor

central incisor

My pediatrician

During my first visit I

My blood group

The first time that I was sick

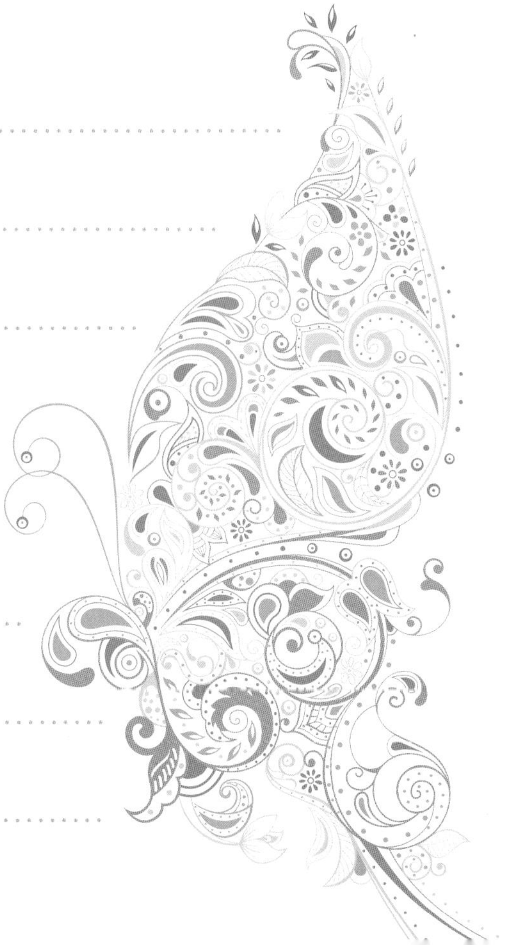

MY FOOTPRINT

MY HANDPRINT

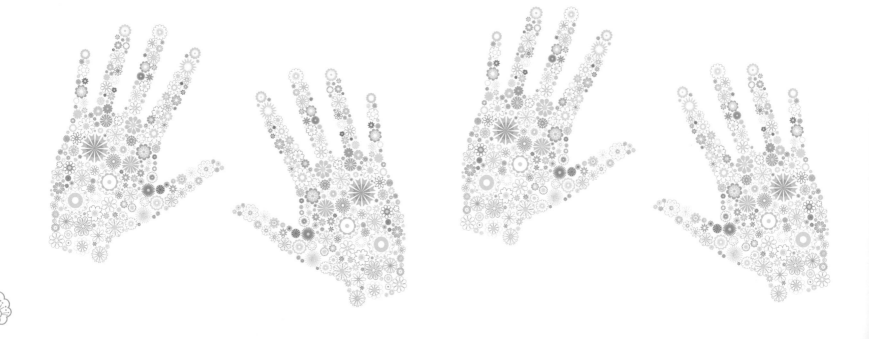

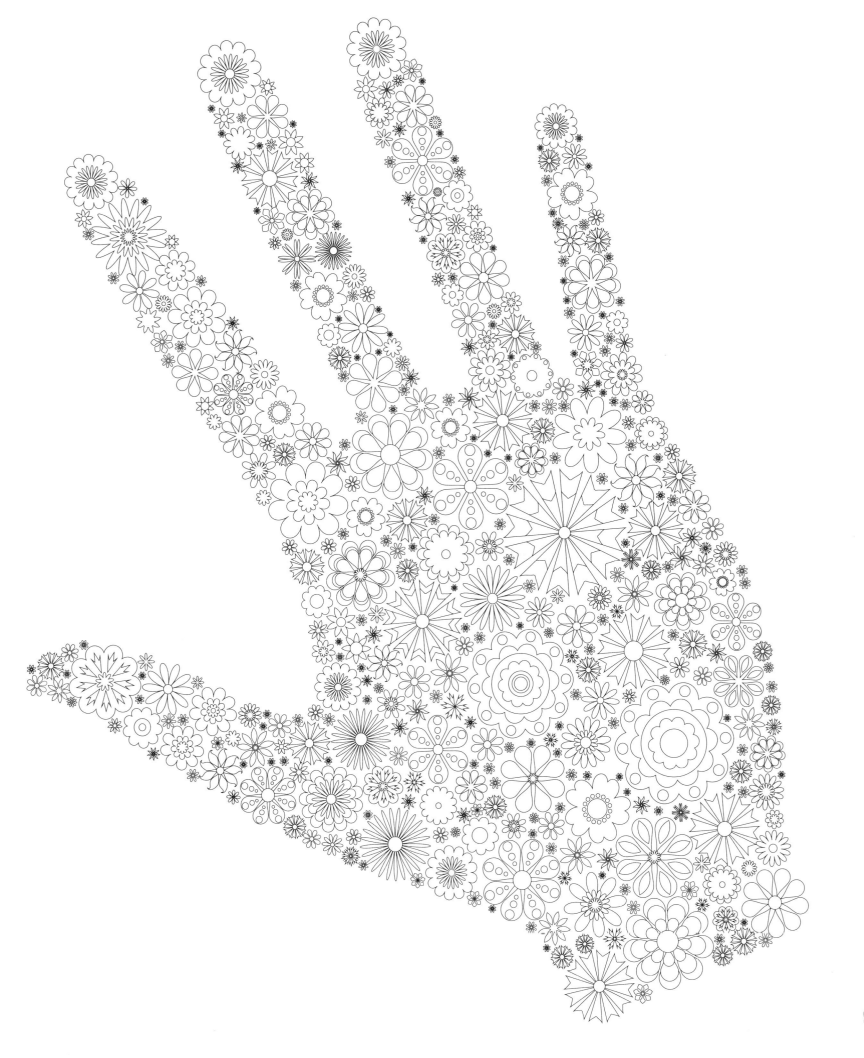

DISCOVERING THE WORLD!

The first family stroll was
....
....
....

This was my reaction
....
....
....
....

The persons I met said the following about me
....
....
....

My favorite places are
....
....
....
....

My family's first vacation
....
....
....

MY PHOTOS

MY FIRST STEPS

I started crawling

....

....

....

I stood up on my own

....

....

....

I took my first steps with a little help

....

....

....

I walked on my own for the first time

....

....

....

I tried running

....

....

....

A SPECIAL OCCASION

The event

....

....

....

....

Who was there

....

....

....

How I behaved

....

....

....

An unforgettable memory

....

....

....

....

A SPECIAL PHOTO

MY PHOTOS

MY FIRST BIRTHDAY

The guests

....

....

....

The cake

....

The gifts

....

....

....

My favorite gift

....

Memories of the party

....

....

....

....

A SPECIAL PHOTO

MY PHOTOS

THE FIRST TIME THAT

I built a tower

....

....

I tried to get dressed on my own

....

....

I ate on my own

....

....

I threw a ball in the air

....

....

I jumped

....

....

My new experiences

....

....

MY FIRST WORDS

My first word was

....

....

I said it

....

....

I said "Mom" for the first time

....

....

I said "Dad" for the first time

....

....

MY FAVORITES

My favorite book

....

....

The toy I never get bored with

....

....

I smile every time I hear this song

....

....

I like playing these games with Mom and Dad

....

....

....

The thing that makes me happier than anything else

....

....

....

The thing that makes me angrier than anything else

....

....

....

What consoles me

....

ON VACATION

Our destination
....

....

How I behaved
....

....

....

....

An unforgettable memory
....

....

....

....

....

....

MY SECOND BIRTHDAY

The guests

....

....

....

The cake

....

The gifts

....

....

....

My favorite gift

....

Memories of the party

....

....

....

....

A SPECIAL PHOTO

MY PHOTOS

THE FIRST TIME THAT

I stopped wearing diapers

....

....

I drew a circle

....

....

I recognized colors

....

....

I counted up to 5

....

....

I brushed my teeth myself

....

....

I rode a tricycle

....

....

I dressed on my own

....

....

I used my own name

....

....

A new experience

....

MY FRIENDS

My friends are called

....

....

....

....

These are the games I play with them

....

....

....

....

MY FAVORITES

My favorite book

....

....

The toy I never get bored with

....

....

I smile every time I hear this song

....

....

I like playing these games with Mom and Dad

....

....

....

The thing that makes me happier than anything else

....

....

....

The thing that makes me angrier than anything else

....

....

....

What consoles me

....

....

A SPECIAL OCCASION

The event
....
....
....
....

Who was there
....
....
....
....

How I behaved
....
....
....
....

An unforgettable memory
....
....
....
....

A SPECIAL PHOTO

MY THIRD BIRTHDAY

The guests

The cake

The gifts

My favorite gift

Memories of the party

A SPECIAL PHOTO

MY PHOTOS

THE FIRST TIME THAT

I drew a picture of an animal

....

....

I went to a friend's party

....

....

I chose my clothes in the morning

....

....

I wrote my own name

....

....

I stopped using a pacifier

....

AT KINDERGARTEN!

How I reacted the first day at kindergarten

....

....

....

....

The teachers are called

....

....

....

....

My new friends are called

....

....

....

....

My best friend is

....

....

....

A SPECIAL PHOTO

A BORN ARTIST:
MY FIRST MASTERPIECE

PHOTO CREDITS

All illustrations are reworkings of images drawn
from 123RF, iStockphoto and Shutterstock

WHITE STAR PUBLISHERS

WS White Star Publishers® is a registered trademark property of De Agostini Libri S.p.A.

© 2015 De Agostini Libri S.p.A.
Via G. da Verrazano, 15 - 28100 Novara, Italy
www.whitestar.it - www.deagostini.it

ISBN 978-88-544-1023-7
1 2 3 4 5 6   19 18 17 16 15

Printed in China